# JEET KUNE DO

Entering to Trapping to Grappling

by Larry Hartsell

# Acknowledgements

I wish to thank the following for their assistance with the photography: Hal Faulkner, Chris Kent, Alphonso Tamez, Cass Magda, Burt Poe, Steve Connoley, Paul Vunak, Ernie Franko, Tim Tackett, Jr. and Tim Tackett, Sr.

ISBN: 0-86568-051-5
Library of Congress Catalog Number: 84-51053

©1984 by Unique Publications.
All rights reserved.
Published 1984.
Printed in the United States of America.

Front Cover Illustration: Walter Lee
Book Design: Katherina Leung & Ron Wong

 UNIQUE
PUBLICATIONS

4201 Vanowen Place
Burbank, California 91505

# Contents

To the memory of Bruce Lee, who was my sifu and my inspiration.

To Linda Lee for her support and introduction.

To Adrian Marshall for his guidance and friendship.

To Dan Inosanto, my sifu, mentor, and above all my friend.

To Richard Bustillo, Jerry Poteet, and the rest of the old Chinatown group with whom I was fortunate enough to train.

To my mother and father who have supported me through good times and bad.

To Tim Tackett, my friend and JKD brother.

*Laurence Benjamin Hartsell*

# Foreword

During the early years of Bruce's stay in the United States, there were just a handful of dedicated martial artists with whom Bruce associated, worked out, and exchanged ideas. This was indeed a quality group, individuals who to this day practice and live the highest ideals of the martial arts and exhibit an awareness of the very simple—yet highly effective—principles of jeet kune do.

Larry Hartsell has been a member of this group, as well as a family friend, to this day. His book, highly regarded by his peers, is a straightforward example of the direct application of jeet kune do to grappling techniques. Larry's book also displays a recognition of the basic concept of jeet kune do, that is, the ability to discriminate between those techniques that are useful to the individual and those that are personally unsuitable.

Bruce would have been proud of Larry's continued growth in the arts and of his constant striving to reach his fullest potential. Writing this book is one step along the way to Larry's greater self-actualization and one, I feel, that Bruce would heartily endorse.

*Linda Lee*

# Dan Inosanto
# WHAT IS JEET KUNE DO?

Jeet kune do—the literal translation is "way of the intercepting fist"—was conceived by Bruce Lee in 1967. Unlike many other martial arts, there are neither a series of rules nor a classification of techniques which constitute a distinct jeet kune do (JKD) method of fighting. JKD is unbound; JKD is freedom. It possesses everything, yet in itself is possessed by nothing. Those who understand JKD are primarily interested in its powers of liberation when JKD is used as a mirror for self-examination.

In the past, many have tried to define JKD in terms of a distinct style: Bruce Lee's kung-fu; Bruce Lee's karate; Bruce Lee's kickboxing; Bruce Lee's system of street fighting. To label JKD "Bruce Lee's martial art" is to completely mistake Bruce Lee's —and JKD's—meaning. JKD's concepts simply cannot be confined within a single system. To understand this, a martial artist must transcend the duality of "for" and "against," reaching for that point of unity which is beyond mere distinction. The understanding of JKD is the direct intuition of this point of unity. According to Bruce Lee, knowledge in the martial arts ultimately means self-knowledge.

Jeet kune do is not a new style of kung-fu or karate. Bruce Lee did not invent a new or composite style, nor did he modify a style to set it apart from any existing method. His concept was to free his followers from clinging to *any* style, pattern, or mold.

It must be emphasized that jeet kune do is merely a name, a mirror reflecting ourselves. There is a sort of progressive approach to JKD training, but as Lee observed: "To create a method of fighting is like putting a pound of water into wrapping paper and shaping it." Structurally, many people mistake JKD as a composite style of martial art because of its efficiency. At any given time jeet kune do can resemble Thai boxing or wing chun or wrestling or karate. Its weaponry resembles Filipino escrima and kali; in long-range application it can resemble Northern Chinese kung-fu or savate.

According to Lee, the efficiency of any style depends upon circumstances and the fighting range of distance: the soldier employs a hand grenade at 50 yards, but he chooses a dagger for close-quarters combat. A staff, to take another example, is the wrong weapon to take to a fight in a telephone booth; a knife would again be the most appropriate weapon.

Jeet kune do is neither opposed or unopposed to the concept of style. We can say that it is outside as well as inside of all particular structures. Because JKD makes no claim to existing as a style, some individuals conclude that it is neutral or indifferent to the question. Again, this is not the case, for JKD is at once "this" and "not this."

A good JKD practitioner rests his actions on direct intuition. According to Lee, a style should never be like the Bible in which the principles and laws can never be violated. There will always be differences between individuals in regard to the quality of training, physical make-up, level of understanding, environmental conditioning, and likes and dislikes. According to Bruce, truth is a "pathless road"; thus JKD is not an organization or an institution of which one can be a member. "Either you understand or you don't—and that is that," he said.

When Bruce taught a Chinese system of kung-fu (it was shortly after his arrival in the United States), he did operate an institute of learning; but after that early period he abandoned his belief in any particular system or style, Chinese or otherwise. Lee did say that to reach the masses one should probably form some type of organization; for his own part, he dismissed the notion as unnecessary to his own teaching. Still, to reach the ever growing numbers of students, some sort of preconceived sets had to be established. And as a result of such a move by martial arts organizations, many of their members would be conditioned to a prescribed system; many of their members would end up as prisoners of systematic drilling.

This is why Lee believed in teaching only a few students at any time. Such a method of instruction required the teacher to maintain an alert observation of each student in order to establish the necessary student-teacher relationship. As Lee so often observed, "A good instructor functions as a pointer of the truth, exposing the student's vulnerability, forcing him to explore himself both internally and externally, and finally integrating himself with his being."

Martial arts—like life itself—is in flux, in constant arhythmic movements, in constant change. Flowing with this change is very important. And finally, any JKD man who says that JKD is exclusively JKD is simply not with it. He is still hung up on his own self-enclosing resistance, still anchored to reactionary patterns, still trapped within limitation. Such a person has not digested the simple fact that truth exists outside of all molds or patterns. Awareness is *never* exclusive. To quote Bruce: "Jeet kune do is just a name, a boat used to get one across the river. Once across it is discarded and not to be carried on one's back."

In 1981, the JKD concept was taught in only three places: the Filipino Kali Academy in Torrance, California; in Charlotte, North Carolina (where Larry Hartsell taught a few select students); and in Seattle, Washington (under the direction of Taki Kimura). The bulk of the JKD concept is taught in Torrance, where the school is under the direction of myself and Richard Bustillo. It is organized in accordance with the premise that a JKD man must undergo different experiences. For example, in Phase 1 and Phase 2 classes at the Filipino Kali Academy, students are taught Western boxing and Bruce Lee's method of kick boxing—*jun fan.*

I deeply feel that students should be taught *experiences* as opposed to *techniques.* In other words, a karate practitioner who has never boxed before *needs* to experience sparring with a boxer. What he learns from that experience is up to him. According to Bruce, a teacher is *not* a giver of truth; he is merely a guide to the truth each student must find.

The total picture Lee wanted to present to his pupils was that above everything else, the pupils must find their own way to truth. He never hesitated to say, "Your truth is not my truth; my truth is not yours."

Bruce did not have a blueprint, but rather a series of guidelines to lead one to proficiency. In using training equipment, there was a systematic approach in which one could develop speed, distance, power, timing, coordination, endurance and footwork.

But jeet kune do was not an end in itself for Bruce—nor was it a mere by-product of his martial studies; it was a means to self discovery. JKD was a prescription for personal growth; it was an investigation of freedom—freedom not only to act naturally and effectively in combat, but in life. In life, we absorb what is useful and reject what is useless, and add to experience what is specifically our own. Bruce Lee always wanted his students to experience judo, jujutsu, aikido, Western boxing; he wanted his students to explore Chinese systems of sensitivity like wing chun, to explore the elements of kali, escrima, arnis; to explore the elements of pentjak silat, Thai boxing, savate. He wanted his students to come to an understanding of the strengths and weaknesses of each method.

No art is superior or inferior to any other. That is the object lesson of jeet kune do, to be unbound, to be free: in combat to use no style as style, to use no way as the way, to have no limitation as the only limitation. Neither be for or against a particular style. In other words, jeet kune do "just is."

Or to use the words of a Zen maxim to describe jeet kune do, "In the landscape of spring there is neither better nor worse. The flowering branches grow, some short, some long."

Dan Inosanto

# I. RANGES OF COMBAT

   As we can see from Dan Inosanto's introduction, jeet kune do is hard to define. The important thing to remember is that JKD is not a style or system. There is no special list of jeet kune do techniques. While there is a structure, JKD students are not bound by it. What Bruce Lee was trying to achieve was his students' ultimate liberation from style. Bruce was always worried that if he were no longer around, his students would freeze jeet kune do — which should always be growing, changing, and adapting — into a rigid style. In a phone call to Daniel Lee a few months before his death, Bruce said that an organized jeet kune do school was a poor idea because "students tend to take the agenda for the way and the program for the truth."

   It is extremely difficult to write a book about jeet kune do, since the reader may look at the book and say, "This is jeet kune do;" or he may turn the ideas in this book into rigid laws; or he may look at some of the techniques through the eyes of his own particular style. In writing this book, I simply want to share some of the things that Bruce taught his students. Take what is useful, reject what is useless, add what is specifically your own. In the final analysis, JKD must be felt, not written about. Bruce would have agreed with Chuang Tzu, the fourth century B.C. Taoist philosopher, who said, "If it could be talked about, everyone would have told his brother."

# Kicking range

To understand a particular martial art, look at the range in which it is most efficient. To simplify things, we will consider four separate ranges. The longest range, or the one that requires the most distance between you and your opponent, is the kicking range. The Northern Chinese kung-fu systems and many of the Korean martial arts specialize in this range. The kicks of these styles are usually thrown from a long distance. A Southern kung-fu style like wing chun usually has kicks which are lower and at a closer distance than in a tae kwon do style, but both types of kicks are in the kicking range. Any time you can touch your opponent with your foot, but he cannot touch you with his hand, you are in the kicking range.

# Hand range

Next is the hand range, the range in which your hands can be used to strike your opponent. This range can be divided into two distances, long and short. A boxer with a good jab may want to use his footwork to stay at the jab-cross range. An infighter may try to draw his opponent closer so he can use tight hooks and uppercuts. Some of the Southern kung-fu styles like wing chun specialize in short range punches.

# Trapping hand range

Next is the trapping hand range, which occurs when you are close enought to immobilize your opponent's arms. This range can be considered a transition from long range to grappling range or from long-range boxing to wing chun punching.

**1**

**2**

# Grappling range

Finally, there is the grappling range, the range in which you can throw your opponent, lock his joints, choke him, or immobilize him. This is the range used in judo and Western wrestling. This book will show you how to get to this range and what to do after you get there.

# Grappling

As Dan Inosanto said in "What is Jeet Kune Do?", "The efficiency of a style depends upon circumstances and ranges of distance." Take the case of a boxer against a kicker, or a boxer against a wrestler. In a match between a boxer and a kicker, the kicker will have the advantage if he can maintain the kicking range. Conversely, if a boxer can bridge the gap to hand range he will have the advantage. The same reasoning applies to the case of the boxer against the wrestler. Since they specialize in different ranges, the one who can maintain his range will have the advantage.

In a sense, a boxer's or kicker's or wrestler's forte can also be his limitation if he can't maintain the range in which he is most efficient. Bruce Lee always thought that you should learn to fit into any environment. Remember that in combat you can't always choose your environment or your range. For example, how does someone whose forte is high kicking defend himself if he's in a swimming pool, or on an icy sidewalk, or on a crowded dance floor? Anyone who aspires to be a complete martial artist should learn to be proficient at any range, in any environment, and with any opponent.

Wrestling is probably man's oldest sport and martial art. It is mentioned in both the Old and New Testament. We have evidence that a form of wrestling was practiced in ancient Egypt and Mesopotamia as far back as 3000 B.C. In the epic *Gilgamesh* there is a wrestling match between the Sumerian heroes and Enkidu.

Every country in Europe has had its own form of wrestling. In England, a form of wrestling called Cornwall and Devon has been traced as far back as the fourth century A.D. The first wrestling text in Europe was written as long ago as 1462. In modern times we have seen the growth of two forms of Western wrestling, Greco-Roman and free-style.

In India, a form of grappling existed as far back as 1500 B.C. India has always been famous for its wrestlers. China has Mongolian wrestling, shuai-chiao, and chin-na. Korea has cireum. Burma has naban. Japan has jujutsu, judo, sumo, and aikido. The Philippines has dumog.

The grappling techniques used in jeet kune do are not limited to Eastern or Western methods, but are based on the principles of both. In jeet kune do we use all methods but are bound by none. At the same time, it was never Bruce's aim to take specific techniques from different systems and call them jeet kune do. It was the principle, not the particular technique, that was important to Bruce.

# Why learn grappling?

A person of small stature may say to himself, "Since I only weigh 120 pounds it would be rather stupid to spend a lot of time learning to wrestle when it is most likely that any opponent I face will probably be much stronger and heavier than I am." At first glance it may seem that the intelligent thing to do is to stay out of reach of a larger opponent. But there are many times that this may not be possible. Remember, you can't always pick your environment. Learning how to wrestle is your first step to learning to defend yourself at grappling range. If you're a police officer, you may be required to control rather than hit an unruly suspect. There may be an occasion when a friend who has had too much to drink wants to test your karate. In this case it's probably better to control him than to take his eye out with a finger jab. If someone on PCP attacks you, he probably will not be stopped by your side kick or reverse punch. You'd better know how to choke a man out.

There are also some occasions when grappling is not a particularly good idea, as when you have more than one opponent. The three essentials are: learn to fit into any range; feel instantly what tool will work at the range in which you happen to find yourself; and try to maintain the optimum range for the particular situation you're in. Finally, remember the old gypsy saying, "Sometimes you get the bear. Sometimes the bear gets you." There are, after all, no sure things.

# II. STANCE AND FOOTWORK

In this chapter we will work on the tools necessary to go from a position out of range to kicking range or grappling range. In jeet kune do we use only one stance, the by-jong stance.

# The by-jong stance

The by-jong stance is not a deep, powerful stance like a horse stance. It is a stance that concentrates on mobility. A wide stance is fine in a karate tournament where your opponent is not allowed to side kick your knee, but in the street you'd better be able to move. Your feet must be far enough apart so that your stance is not too weak, yet not so wide that you can't move. The exact distance is up to the individual. Your feet should be at a 45 degree angle, and your hands up, covering your center line. Once you have a stance that feels comfortable, you can begin to work on footwork. While there are over 24 different footwork patterns in JKD, we will concentrate only on those that will move us from long range to grappling range.

The following examples of footwork should be used for entering from out of range to kicking or hand range.

# The step and slide-shuffle advance

The step and slide shuffle is just what it sounds like. You take a step forward with your front foot, then slide your rear foot forward to return to your original stance. Your front foot can step forward any distance from one inch to one foot, depending on the space between you and your opponent. This footwork is not used to deliver a hand or foot strike but rather for getting closer to your opponent, to bridge the gap, to enter.

**1**

**2**

**3**

# Slide-shuffle advance

The slide-shuffle advance is the opposite of the step and slide. In the slide shuffle, your rear foot will slide forward, then your front steps up, returning you to your original stance. Depending on the distance you need to travel, your rear foot can move forward any distance from one inch to all the way past your front leg. The slide shuffle is usually used to deliver a kick. It will take you into kicking range.

1

2

3

# Lead step forward with slide-shuffle advance

This is a combination of the above two footwork patterns and is used to gain more distance. Step forward with the front foot and then perform a slide shuffle advance.

**1**

**2**

**3**

**4**

# Push shuffle

The push shuffle looks like a step and slide shuffle advance but is quite different. To perform a push shuffle, you push off the rear leg to thrust your front foot forward. This returns you to your original stance. This technique is used to deliver a hand attack.

The following types of footwork are used in grappling.

**1**

**2**

**3**

# Curve right (or left)

The curve right is used to move from outside your opponent's front leg to the inside position. From the tie-up position, slide your front foot back, then step up and inside his front foot. The curve left is done the same way, only you start in a left forward stance.

**1**

**2**

**3**

# Replace step on the inside line

To switch leads in the tie-up position, simply step forward with your rear leg, then step back with your right while staying inside your opponent's front foot.

**1**

**2**

**3**

# Replace step from inside to outside

Step forward with your rear (left) foot to outside your opponent's front foot, then step back with your right.

**1**

**2**

**3**

# Step through

To unbalance your opponent, step forward with your rear (right) leg while shoving forward with your right shoulder.

**1**

**2**

# Triangle pattern

Another way to go from the inside to the outside line while switching your lead leg is by using triangle footwork. When you have a left leg lead, slide your left leg back to your right leg. Then step out with your left leg and slide your right leg to your left. Finally step forward with your right foot.

**1**

**2**

**5**

**3**

**4**

# Circling

To move behind your opponent, step forward with your left leg, then step forward with your right foot. This puts you to the outside of the opponent. Finally step around and behind with your left.

While these are examples of only some of the footwork used in JKD, mastering them will allow you to perform all the techniques used in this book.

**1**

**2**

**3**

**4**

# III. TOOLS FOR TRAPPING

Say you throw a hand attack and your opponent blocks it. To continue your attack, you either have to change the line of your attack or remove the barrier which his block creates. If you remove the barrier, you should try to immobilize it so he can't use it again. When you have immobilized it, you've trapped it.

Before you learn specific traps you'll need to understand some reference points.

**1** Trapping, both hands facing out.

**2** Trapping, right hand inside, left hand outside.

**3** Trapping, both hands facing inside, wide.

**4** Trapping, both hands facing inside, tight.

**5** Trapping, right hand outside, left hand inside.

Your arms can meet your opponent's arms in a number of different combinations: both hands facing out, right to right; right hand inside and left hand outside; both hands facing inside wide; both hands inside tight; right hand outside and left hand inside; and both hands outside left to left. The way your arms meet dictates what traps or combinations of traps will be the most effective.

Much of the jeet kune do trapping hands come from wing chun. JKD differs from wing chun in its follow-ups. Since jeet kune do students traditionally use wing chun terminology, we will use it for many of the traps.

When you hit your opponent, he can answer your attack (block) with either his front or rear hand. A karate man will usually answer (block) with his front hand while a boxer will usually answer (parry) with his rear hand.

The following techniques can be used against a front hand high answer.

# Pak sao (slap hand)

If your opponent blocks your front hand with his front hand, slap his front forearm with your rear hand. This will remove the front hand barrier and let you renew your attack. Use the push-shuffle forward to maintain the proper distance.

**1**

**2**

**3**

# Pak sao to pak sao

If you use a pak sao on your opponent's front hand and he responds with a rear hand parry you can remove the barrier by slapping the inside of his wrist with your rear hand and punching again.

**1**

**2**

**3**

# Pak sao to lop sao (grab hand)

For another counter to his rear hand parry, you can lop (grab) his wrist and hit him with a back fist.

**1**

**2**

# Pak sao to wedge to pak sao

For another counter, you can wedge with your rear hand, use a pak sao with your front hand, and hit with your rear hand.

**1**

**2**

**3**

# Lop sao to lop sao

If your opponent gives you a front hand answer, you can lop his front hand and throw a back fist. If he parries that, you can lop again and punch.

**1**

**2**

**4**

**3**

**5**

# Lop sao to small disengagement to lop sao

If you lop and launch a straight punch, and he cross-parries your punch, you can disengage your hand and move it to the outside line. This will allow you to lop his rear hand and hit.

**1**

**4**

**2**

**3**

**5**

**6**

# Lop sao to pak sao

If you lop your opponent's front hand with your front hand and punch with your rear, he may raise his front arm and block your punch. In this case, pak with the hand you used to punch, thus opening the line so you can punch with your front hand.

**1**

**2**

**3**

**4**

# Pak sao to lop sao

If you try to pak with your rear hand and punch with your front hand, he may raise his front arm. In that case, you can lop with your front hand and punch with your rear.

**1**

**2**

**3**

**4**

# Jao sao (circling hand) to jut sao (jerking hand)

If your opponent blocks your front hand with his front arm you can use a jao sao (circling palm hit). If he blocks, you can jut by jerking his arm down and punching.

**1**

**2**

**3**

**4**

If he blocks your punch you can press his arm down and punch with your opposite hand.

**5**

**6**

# Jao sao to punch

If your opponent blocks your jao sao with his front arm, he will have opened up his center line and you can hit him with your rear hand.

**1**

**2**

**3**

# High jao sao to low jao sao to pak sao and back fist

If your opponent blocks your high jao sao, you can also switch your attack to the lower line by hitting him with a jao sao to the groin. You can then pak his front hand and back fist.

**1**

**2**

**3**

**4**

**5**

**6**

# High jao sao to small disengagement to neck grab with punch and elbow

If your opponent blocks your high jao sao, you can circle your hand to the inside line. You can then grab his neck and punch him, following up your attack by striking him with your right elbow.

**1**

**2**

**3**

**4**

**5**

**6**

**7**

**8**

The following technique can be used against a low front hand answer.

# Pak sao to back fist

If you jab low and your opponent blocks with his front hand, pak sao his front arm and back fist.

**1**

**2**

**3**

Finally, here's a technique to use for a low rear hand answer.

# Jao sao

If your opponent blocks your low jab with his rear hand you can jao sao to the high line.

**1**

**2**

**3**

# IV. ENTERING TO TRAPPING TO GRAPPLING

This chapter will show you ways to bridge the gap and go from kicking range to hand range to grappling range. Once you have the concept, your techniques will be limited only by your imagination.

# Shin kick to finger jab

From the outside range, bridge the gap with a shin kick using a slide shuffle advance. Step down while executing a finger jab. If your opponent blocks with his front hand, lop sao and punch while bringing your left leg and shoulder forward. When you lop, make sure his elbow is up. Bring him to the ground by pressing on his elbow with your forearm as you pull up on his wrist. At the same time step forward with your left leg. To control him, kneel on his arm, and pin him to the ground.

**1**

**2**

**5**

**3**

**4**

**6**

# Small disengagement to side-strangle and throw

Another sequence to use when your opponent blocks your finger jab is to circle your hand to the inside while you lift up on his right elbow with your left hand. Curve to the left and push-shuffle forward. You should end up with your leg behind his front leg. Strangle him by squeezing with your forearm and shoulder. You can also throw him by reaping with your front leg.

1

2

5

**3**

**4**

# Single leg attack on the inside to back trip

Another response to your opponent's jab is to step forward, bend down, and pick up his front leg. This must be done quickly, before he can counter with a downward elbow strike. Once you've picked up his leg, quickly step behind his rear leg. Throw him by pushing on his hip as you lift up on his ankle.

1

2

3

4

# Leg spread control with toe hold

You can control your opponent by twisting his ankle as you step on his inner thigh.

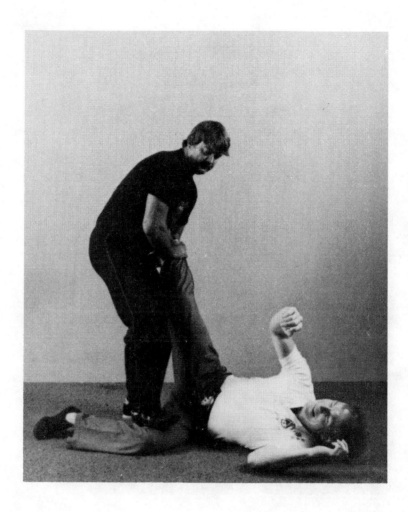

# Step over toe hold

You can also control him by twisting his ankle as you step over his leg and roll him over onto his stomach. To cause pain, lock and twist his ankle.

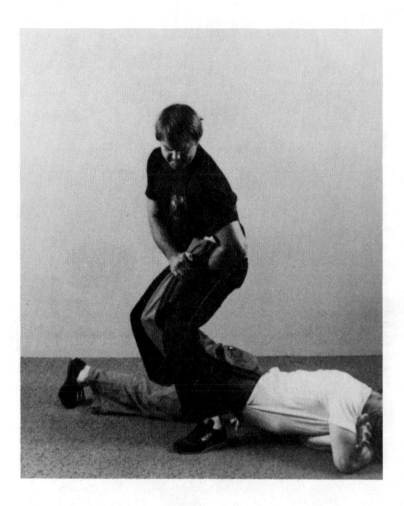

# Rear single leg attack
# to kneeling leg lock

If your opponent uses a rear single leg attack, step behind with your left leg as you pick up his front ankle with your right arm. Unbalance him by pushing his shoulder with your left hand, and then throw him by pulling up on his leg and pushing down on his hip with your left forearm. To control your opponent, lock his leg as you kneel down on the back of his knee.

1

**2**

**3**

**4**

# Rear single leg attack to sitting leg lock

You can use a sitting leg lock on your opponent instead of the kneeling lock just shown. After throwing him, step over his right leg with your left leg. Lock his leg by sitting down on the back of his knee and pushing forward with your right hand.

**1**

**2**

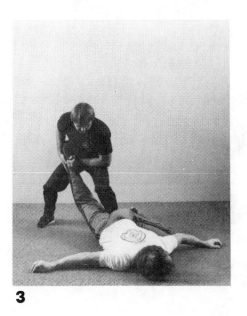

**3**

**4**

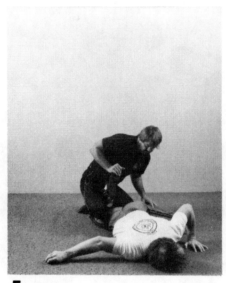

**5**

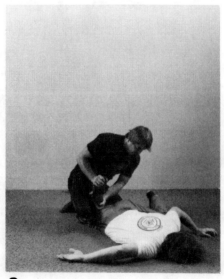

**6**

# Ankle pick-up on inside with groin smash

When your opponent jabs, step forward with your right foot while picking up his ankle with your left hand. You can bring him to the ground by smashing his groin with your right palm. Finish him off by dropping your knee to his groin.

**1**

**2**

**3**

**4**

# Finger jab to hook kick to finger jab

Another entry technique sequence is the finger jab to hook kick to finger jab. Step forward and throw a finger jab to your opponent's right eye. Slide up with your rear leg and hook kick his groin. Then step down and jab to his eye again.

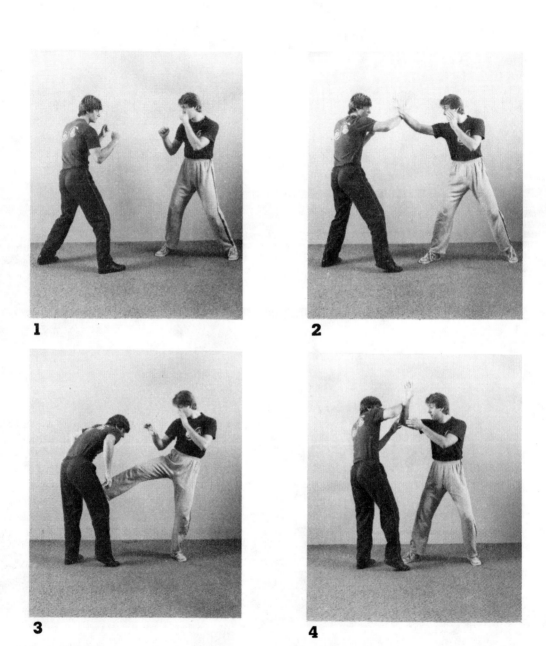

1

2

3

4

The following show some of the many follow-ups you can use if your opponent blocks your final finger jab.

# Double leg takedown

Bend forward and throw your opponent by picking up his legs
as you shove forward with your right shoulder.

**1**

**2**

# Double leg lock

Control your opponent by pinning his ankles under your armpits and lifting up.

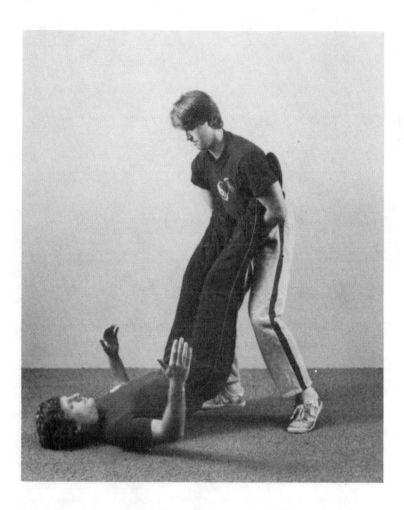

# Sitting scissors control

You can follow up the standing leg lock by sitting down, then scissoring your opponent's legs.

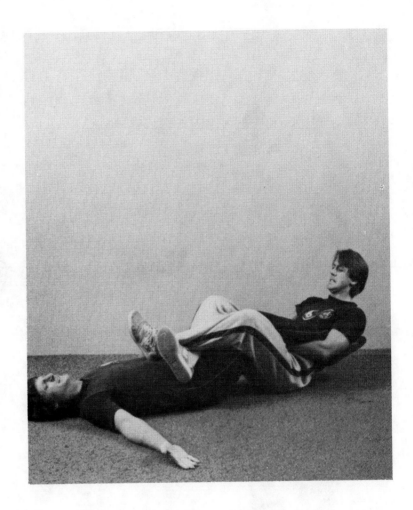

# Figure four arm lock

Grasp your opponent's right wrist with your right hand, reach through, and grab your own right forearm with your left hand. To throw your opponent to the ground, step forward with your left leg and smash his right shoulder with your right elbow.

**1**

**2**

**3**

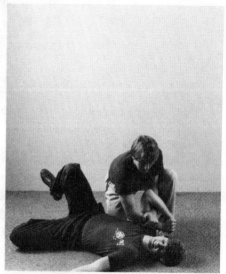

**4**

# Bent arm lever

Grasp your opponent's right wrist with you left hand. Bring your right arm under your joined arms, and grasp your own left wrist with your right hand. To throw your opponent, bend his arm down as you step forward with your left leg and kneel on your right knee.

1

2

3

4

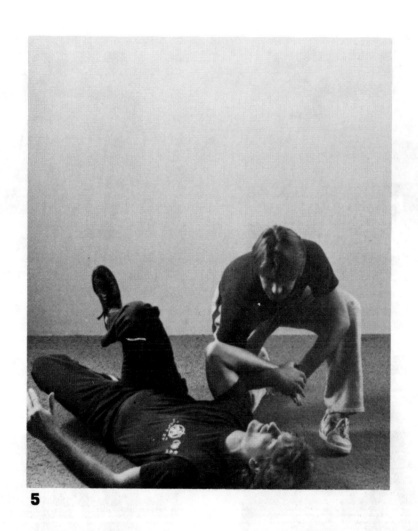

**5**

# Pak sao to reverse figure-four headlock

Pak sao your opponent with your left palm as you strike his neck with your right forearm. Wrap your right arm around his head, twisting it clockwise under your armpit. Place your left arm on top of his neck and apply pressure by lifting up.

**1**

**2**

**3**

**4**

**5**

# Low jab entry

When used as a feeler or a fake, the low jab can be an efficient entry technique.

Step forward with your right foot and fake a low jab to your opponent's floating rib. Make sure you cover your head with your left hand.

**1**

**2**

# Pak sao and back hand chop

If your opponent blocks with his front hand, pak sao with your left hand and throw a back hand chop to his neck. If he doesn't react to your low fake, simply hit him.

# Inside pak sao and punch to
# head butt to reaping throw

If your opponent blocks your back hand chop with his rear hand, inside pak his left arm with your left palm. At the same time throw a vertical fist punch to his nose, chin, or throat with your right fist. Grasp his neck with your right arm and pull him forward into a head butt. Then step behind him and bring him down with a reaping throw.

**3**

**4**

**1**

**2**

**5**

# Low fake to backhand chop to arm take down

This follow-up to the low fake and back hand chop comes from the Filipino martial art of kali. If your opponent blocks your backhand chop with his rear hand, strike his biceps with your right elbow and grasp his left forearm with your left hand. Next, throw him by stepping on his foot while you step back with your rear foot. Simultaneously, push down on his arm and twist your body counterclockwise.

**1**

**2**

**3**

**4**

**5**

**6**

Use the following techniques if you fake a low jab and your opponent blocks with his rear hand.

# Jao sao to head butt to rear strangle throw

This time when you fake low, cover your opponent's right wrist with your left hand. Jao sao with a palm strike to your opponent's left ear, grasp his neck, and head butt. Then step behind and throw him over your leg as you strangle him.

**1**

**2**

**3**

**4**

**5**

**6**

# Small disengagement to side-strangle throw

Circle your right hand to the inside of your opponent's left arm. Lift his right elbow and place it on your right shoulder. Then throw him to the ground and strangle him.

**1**

**2**

**3**

**4**

**5**

**6**

**7**

**8**

The next sequences show the high jab entry.

# Jab to pak sao to forearm smash with reaping throw

This is one of Bruce Lee's favorite throws. After you jab and pak sao, use the slide shuffle advance as you grasp your opponent's hair with your right hand. Smash his nose with your forearm and throw him.

**1**

**2**

**5**

**6**

**3**

**4**

**7**

After you've thrown him you can control him with an arm bar across your thigh, or you can finish him off by dropping your knee on his stomach and poking his eye.

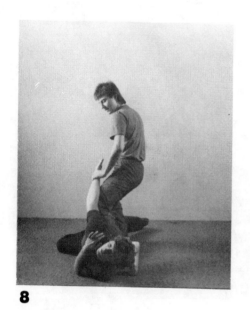

**8**

**9**

After the jab and pak sao you can also use any of the following techniques.

# Front sweep throw

Pivot your right foot to the outside of your opponent's right foot as you raise your left leg. Throw him by pushing his right shoulder, pulling his right wrist, and sweeping his right leg.

1

2

3

Control him by kneeling on his elbow as you lift up on his wrist, or by doing a sit-down arm lock.

**4**

**5**

# Jab to lop sao to forearm to throat with rear kicking sweep throw to elbow finish

Jab, then lop sao as you punch with your left hand. Bring your left hand to your right shoulder. Throw your opponent by kicking his right leg as you smash his throat with your left forearm. Finish him off with an elbow to his neck.

**1**

**3**

**2**

**4**

**5**

**6**

# Jab to Pak sao and punch to lop sao and back fist to cradle throw with knee drop

Jab and pak sao as you punch again with your right hand. If your opponent blocks your punch, lop sao his right arm as you throw a left back fist to his temple. Step behind him as you bring your left arm across his throat. To throw him, simply pick him up. While keeping control of his left leg, finish him off by dropping your left knee onto his floating rib.

**1**

**2**

**3**

**4**

**5**

**6**

**7**

The following technique starts in an unmatched stance—
you're in a right lead while your opponent is in a left lead.

# Jab to inverted hook kick to foot stomp to chin hit to arm lock with front sweep throw

When your opponent blocks your jab, do a slide shuffle advance as you throw an inverted hook kick to your opponent's groin. After the kick, stomp down on his front foot. Bring your right arm under his left as you strike his chin with your left palm. Step in front of his front leg, and then bend him forward and over your leg by levering his left arm as you push down on the back of his neck. Throw him by sweeping his front foot with your front foot.

**1**

**2**

**3**

**4**

**5**

**6**

**7**

# Jab to step through hook kick to neck and hip throw

If your opponent blocks your jab, throw a rear leg hook kick, hitting your opponent's front thigh with your shin. Step down, and hit the back of his neck with your palm. Return to your stance, and strike his throat with your right forearm. At the same time, push his hip with your left palm. After his balance is broken, throw him by dropping onto your right knee, and finish him off with a stranglehold.

**1**

**2**

**3**

**4**

**5**

**6**

**7**

The following technique uses the jab cross entry.

# Jab-cross to rear leg front push kick to drop knee to foot with push knee throw

The jab-cross entry comes from boxing, while the follow-up shown here comes from kali. This is a good example of mixing two different martial arts. After your cross, raise your rear leg and perform a front push kick to your opponent's hip as you grab his right arm with your left. Step down with your left leg and drop your right knee onto his instep. Throw him by pushing his knee.

**1**

**2**

**3**

**4**

**5**

**6**

**7**

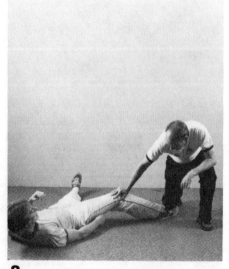

**8**

# V. GRAPPLING AS A DEFENSE

Grappling can be used as a defense as well as an offense. This chapter will deal with some of the grappling techniques you can use against a punch or a kick.

First we will look at defenses against a jab.

# Outside parry to ear slap to side standing strangle

When your opponent jabs, slip to the outside and parry with your rear hand. At the same time, slap his ear with your palm. Push-shuffle behind him as you raise his right arm. From this position you can strangle him by pressing your forearm into the side of his neck.

1

2

3

4

# Outside parry with ear slap
# to drop-knee strangle

As you start your side-standing strangle, pivot behind your opponent, drop his spine down onto your knee, and strangle him by pressing your forearm across his throat.

1

2

3

4

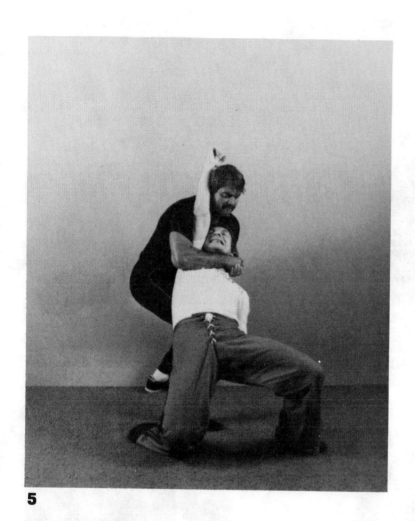

**5**

# Catch to figure-four arm lock to takedown

When your opponent jabs, catch his fingers in the palm of your rear hand. Grasp his right wrist with your left hand as he starts to retract his jab. At the same time, bring your right arm on top of his elbow to grasp your own left forearm. Slide shuffle and throw him with a leg sweep as you lever his arm towards the floor.

**1**

**2**

**3**

**4**

**5**

# Catch to underarm lock to switch

Catch your opponent's jab in your rear palm. Bring your right arm under and to the outside of his right. Grasp your own wrist as you bend his arm down. Switch with a replace step and control him by pinning his right arm under your left.

1

2

3

4

**5**

# Outside parry to forearm-hit to inside elbow to elbow-wrist takedown to wrist lock control

This is also a technique from kali. As your opponent jabs, parry his punch from the outside and smash down on the inside of his right elbow with your right. Throw him to the ground by twisting his wrist while pushing down on his elbow. Meanwhile, twist your body counterclockwise and drop to your knee.

1

2

3

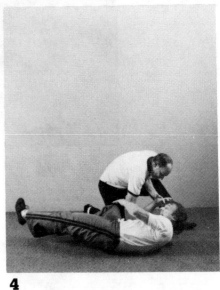

4

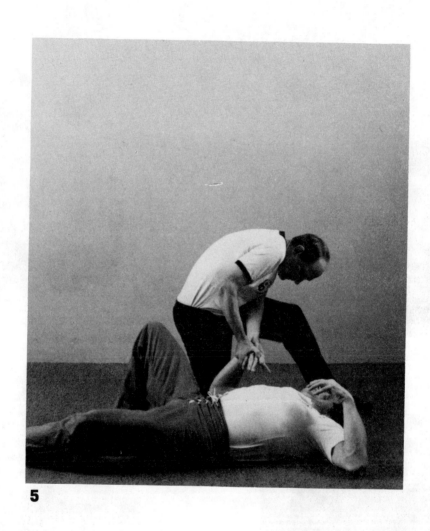

**5**

The following are defenses against a jab cross.

# Catch and bong sao to arm lock

Catch your opponent's jab in your rear hand. When he crosses, deflect his punch with a bong sao block from wing chun. Lop sao with your rear hand. Step out with your right leg as you twist his arm so that the elbow is facing up. Bring him to the ground by pressing down just above his elbow with your left forearm.

**1**

**2**

**3**

**4**

**5**

# Catch, bong sao to arm
# drag with front trip

After your bong sao, lop your opponent's rear arm with your rear hand. Throw him by shuffling up and kicking his legs out from under him. At the same time push down on the back of his head and lift up on his arm.

**1**

**2**

**3**

**4**

**5**

**6**

**7**

# Catch to shoulder-roll elbow block to double-leg tackle throw to double-leg lock spine stretch

Catch your opponent's jab with your rear hand. When he crosses, twist your hip slightly to the right and deflect the punch with your right elbow or forearm. Pick up both of his legs. Once he's on the ground, apply pressure by lifting up on his legs. Then roll him over and straddle him, lifting up on his legs as you lean back.

1

2

3

4

**5**

**6**

**7**

**8**

# Shoulder stop to behind the neck arm break to rear choke

When your opponent throws a wild roundhouse punch (typical of the barroom brawl punch), stop the punch by hitting his punching shoulder with your front palm. At the same time, block the punch with your rear hand. Grab his wrist and lift his arm as you step forward with your rear leg. Simultaneously, place your left arm across his neck. Hyperextend his elbow by bending his arm across the back of your neck. Then pivot around and apply a rear strangle.

1

2

3

4

**5**

# Inside parry with finger jab to hand choke and back trip

Instead of hitting your opponent's shoulder, throw a finger jab to his right eye. Then shuffle up as you grab his windpipe and his left wrist. Throw him by first breaking his balance and then trip him over your leg as you push down on his throat. Once he's on the ground, control him by bending his arm across your thigh as you continue to apply your hand choke.

**1**

**2**

**3**

**4**

**5**

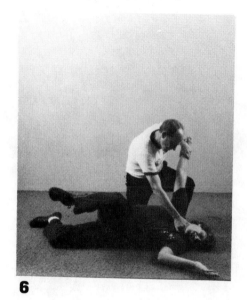

**6**

# Shoulder stop to forearm to throat with arm blast to shoulder drag and hair-pull throw

When your opponent hooks, use a shoulder stop, then slam your forearm into the side of his neck. Use your right forearm to blast his arm down. Bring your arm across the top of his arm, then circle your left arm clockwise to a straight arm lock. Grab his hair and drive his face into the ground by stepping back and kneeling. You can then control him with a straight arm lock or finish him off with a hammer fist to the back of his neck.

**1**

**2**

**3**

**4**

**5**

**6**

**9**

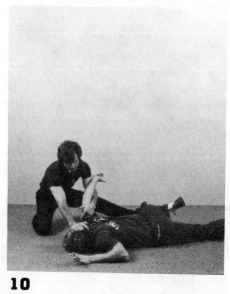

**10**

**7**

**8**

**11**

# Shoulder stop to half nelson arm-drag throw with cross-arm neck control

After your shoulder stop, push your opponent's chin back with your palm, and smash his jaw with a right hammer fist. Replace step as you grab his right wrist with your right hand. Next, throw an uppercut punch under his right arm, and reach around to grab his neck with your left hand. Throw him by pushing down on his neck and arm. To control him, wrap his right arm across his throat and press down.

**1**

**2**

**5**

**6**

**3**

**4**

**7**

**8**

**9**

**10**

**13**

**11**

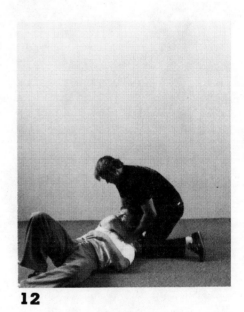

**12**

# Shoulder stop with arm
# blast to rear choke

After you shoulder stop, blast your opponent's arm down. Step behind your left leg and apply a choke.

**1**

**2**

**5**

**3**

**4**

# Shoulder stop to arm to groin lever

This time, after your shoulder stop, bring his attacking arm down between his legs. Holding his arm with your right, step behind and grasp his wrist with your left hand. Control him by pushing down on his back as you pull up on his arm.

**1**

**2**

**5**

**6**

**3**

**4**

# Bob-and-weave to single-leg pick-up with side kick takedown to bent-leg control

When your opponent hooks, bob forward and to the right. Weave under his punch as you hook his ribs. Step up with your front leg, grab his right ankle, and pick his leg up as you press on his hip with your forearm. Bring him to the ground by throwing a side kick at his supporting leg. Control him by bending his leg across your arm.

1

2

5

6

**3**

**4**

**7**

**8**

# Bob-and-weave with double hook to neck crank

Bob and weave under your opponent's hook. As you weave, twist your body to gain power and throw a hook to his jaw. Step around and twist violently to your right.

There are a number of defenses against the hook (roundhouse kick). In jeet kune do we call what is commonly known as a roundhouse kick a hook kick because it follows the same line as a hook punch.

**1**

**2**

**5**

**6**

**3**

**4**

**7**

# Double block to shelf and cradle foot with foot pin throw

Catch your opponent's hook kick by bringing your left arm down and your right arm across your body. Then bring your left arm up and around to capture his foot, and step forward onto his front foot. To throw him, grab his hair and shove forward while stepping forward with your left leg. You can finish him off with a knee strike or punch.

1

2

5

**3**

**4**

# Shelf to step-over leg lock with single spinal stretch

Shelf your opponent's hook kick by circling with your rear arm, and capturing his leg against your upper arm. Bend his leg by pulling him toward you. To throw him, step forward and shove with your right arm. Step over his leg with your left leg, and then sit down on his thigh. Control him by bending his leg over your thigh.

**1**

**2**

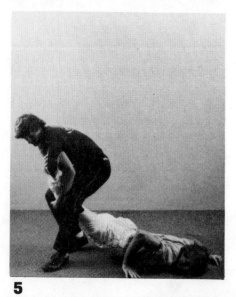

**5**

**6**

**3**

**4**

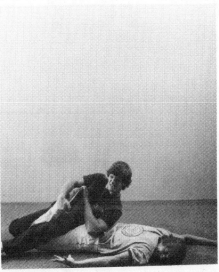

**7**

Here are some defenses against the heel hook kick.

# Step-in shelf to leg takedown with a reverse sitting leg lock

Step forward and slightly to the left inside his heel. Shelf his leg with your right arm. Shuffle forward as you push his hip. At the same time, step in front of his leg. When he is on the ground, step over his leg with your left leg. Twist to your right and sit down. You can control him by bending his leg over your right thigh. Note that in this technique sequence, the opponents start from an unmatched stance.

**1**

**2**

**5**

**6**

**3**

**4**

# Step-in shelf with lifting
# leg throw to knee

As your opponent throws a heel hook, step in and shelf with
your right arm. Pick him up and throw him by twisting to your left.
To finish him off, drop your knee onto his stomach. Then twist and
drop your left knee onto his temple.

1

2

5

**3**

**4**

The next technique is a defense against a spinning back kick.

# Stop kick with hair takedown

If your timing is right, you can intercept your opponent's spin kick with a side kick to his hip. Then step down and grab his hair with your right hand. Your left hand can go around his neck to choke him or grab his left shoulder. Step back and kneel onto your left knee to drop his back onto your right knee.

**1**

**2**

**5**

**3**

**4**

And here's a defense against a side kick.

# Down elbow with oblique kick with lifting leg throw to drop knee to groin

As your opponent side kicks, lean back and smash his leg with a downward elbow block. Shelf his leg with your hand and throw an oblique kick to the knee. At the same time, trap his front arm with your front arm, then grab his leg with your front arm. Throw him by stepping to your left as you lift his leg and twist it to the left.

**1**

**2**

**5**

**6**

**3**

**4**

Finally, there is the defense against the front kick.

# Forearm block to step-up shelf to pull back-and-throw to leg lock with leg spread

When your opponent throws a front kick, angle to the right and block with your right forearm. Step up and shelf his leg with your left arm. To throw him, step up as you bend his leg and push down. When he's on the ground, apply a leg lock. At the same time, spread his legs apart with your left leg.

**1**

**2**

**5**

**6**

**3**

**4**

# VI. GRAPPLING FROM THE TIE-UP OR CLINCH POSITION

Grappling most often starts from the tie-up position. This is what we refer to as the grappling range. You can get to a basic tie-up position by using trapping hands or by the use of the clinch, a boxing technique.

From the following tie-up positions you can head butt, strike with the knee or elbow, stomp, bite, gouge, thumb the eye, throw, or lock your opponent.

# Pak sao to inside neck grasp

Pak with your left hand as you push-shuffle forward. Reach with your right hand to grab his neck.

**1**

**2**

# Pak sao to pak sao to inside neck grasp

If your opponent blocks your first pak, grasp his rear hand during your first pak sao, then open the line with a second pak sao.

**1**

**2**

**3**

# Pak to outside neck grasp

This time when you pak sao, twist your arm as if you were throwing a back hand chop and grab your opponent's neck on the outside line.

**1**

**2**

# Pak sao to wedge to lop sao to outside kick grasp

If your opponent blocks your pak sao with his rear hand, wedge by thrusting forward with rear hand palm up. Then lop sao and back fist. After this, grab his neck on the outside line.

**1**

**2**

**5**

**3**

**4**

# Pak sao to lop sao
# to outside neck grasp.

This is the same as "pak sao to wedge to lop sao to outside kick grasp" shown above except that you delete the wedge.

**1**

**2**

**5**

**3**

**4**

# Pak sao to jao sao to neck pull

As you pak sao, throw a jao sao. Then grab your opponent's neck and pull him towards you.

1

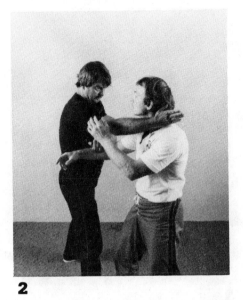

2

3

Next are three examples of going from trapping hands to strangling.

# Pak sao to pak sao to rear strangle

If your opponent blocks your pak sao with his rear hand, pak again and punch. Then execute a strangle.

1

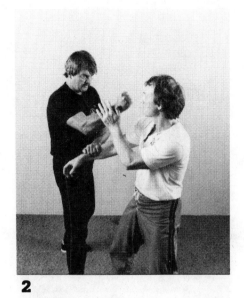

2

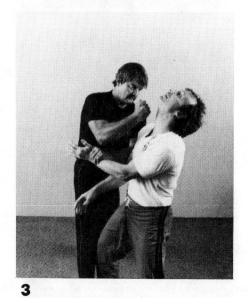

3

4

# Pak sao to pak sao
# to neck-crank strangle

After your second pak sao and punch, go to the outside neck grasp position. Twist your arm clockwise and capture your opponent's head in a neck crank strangle. Apply pressure by lifting up on his neck.

**1**

**2**

**5**

**6**

**3**

**4**

**7**

# Pak sao to small disengagement to standing side-strangle

After your small disengagement, step behind and apply a side-standing strangle.

**1**

**2**

**5**

**3**

**4**

The following are only some of the ways to move from boxing to a clinch or tie-up position.

# Single arm wrap-around

Slip inside your opponent's jab, and uppercut. Then wrap your left arm around your opponent's right arm, and push his left shoulder to prevent his hitting you with his rear hand. Angle to the left to apply pressure on his arm and to zone away from his rear arm. To add more pressure, push on his right shoulder.

1

2

5

6

**3**

**4**

**7**

# Double arm wrap-around

This is the same as the single arm wrap-around, except this time your opponent punches with his rear arm before you can stop his shoulder. Block with your elbow and wrap around, trapping both his arms at the elbow.

**1**

**2**

**5**

**6**

**3**

**4**

**7**

# Single arm wrap-around to neck grasp

After you apply the single arm wrap-around, angle to the left and wrap your right arm around your opponent's neck. Then step behind and apply a strangle hold.

1

2

5

6

**3**

**4**

**7**

# Shoulder stop to shoulder stop to headlock or hip throw

You're in a right leg lead and your opponent attempts a front hand hook. Execute a shoulder stop by hitting his shoulder with the palm of your hand. Then apply a single arm wrap-around. If he tries to hit you with his rear hand or overhand punch, stop his punch with another shoulder stop. Pivot to the right and step out with your left leg. At the same time, wrap your left arm around his neck and twist him over your hip. From this position you can hold him in a headlock or throw him over your hip.

**1**

**2**

**5**

**6**

You can move from **grappling** to a tie up position in many ways. You can get there if your opponent grabs you, or if you grab your opponent. You can also get there from boxing or trapping hand range. Although many martial arts do not stress this range, it is common in **actual combat** and should be practiced.

**3**

**4**

**7**

# Neck and elbow drag throw

Bend to the left. By lowering your shoulder and pulling down on your opponent's arm and neck, throw him to the ground. Keeping your hold on his left arm during the throw. Control him by locking his arm over your leg.

1

2

3

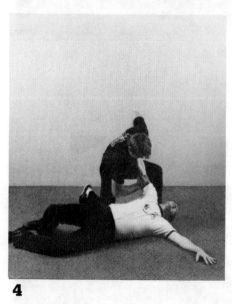

4

# Arm lift to side-standing choke-throw

Lift up on your opponent's elbow and step behind him with your front leg. Throw him over your leg or hip while still applying a choke.

**1**

**2**

**3**

**4**

**5**

# Shoulder push to single-leg takedown

Push your opponent's left shoulder with your right hand. Then bend down and grab his right ankle with your left hand. Pick up his leg as you push on his right hipbone with your right forearm. After he's on the ground, finish him off with a drop knee to his groin.

1

2

3

4

**5**

# Shoulder push with arm lift or rear single-leg takedown to leg lock

After the push shoulder and arm lift, step behind your opponent. Pick up his right ankle as you push down on his hip. This will bring him to the ground. Then step over his leg and apply a leg lock.

**1**

**2**

**3**

**4**

**5**

**6**

**7**

**8**

# Arm lift and single-leg pick-up with trip

Lift your opponent's left arm. Then step up and place your right leg behind his left leg as you grab both of his knees. To throw him, pick up his right leg as you push forward with your shoulders. Control him by trapping and twisting his ankle under your arm.

**1**

**2**

**3**

**4**

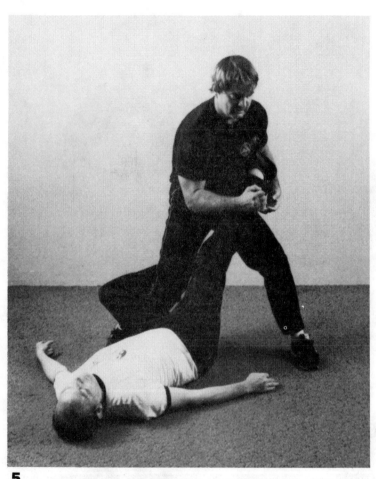

**5**

# Cradle throw

Lift your opponent's arm. While keeping your hold on his right arm, bend and grab his right thigh. Straighten up and throw him over your left shoulder. Finish him off with two knee drops.

**1**

**2**

**3**

**4**

**5**

**6**

# Step-on-foot to knee-push

Step forward with your right leg and step on your opponent's right foot. Throw him to the ground by pushing on his knee with both palms.

**1**

**2**

**3**

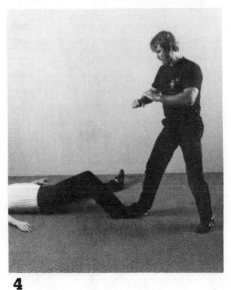

**4**

# Knee lock and push

Step forward with your right foot behind your opponent's right foot. To throw him, pull on his left arm, push on his neck, and push forward with your right leg.

1

2

3

# Palming to double-leg takedown with double-leg lock and spine stretch

Shove your opponent's chin back with your right palm. Bend down, grab his knees and tackle him by picking him up and shoving forward with your shoulder. After he's on the ground, slide your arms up and trap his feet. Then roll him over and sit down.

1

2

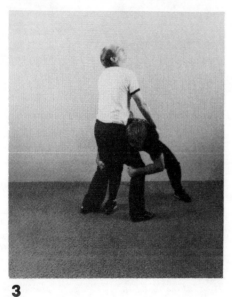

3

4

**5**

**6**

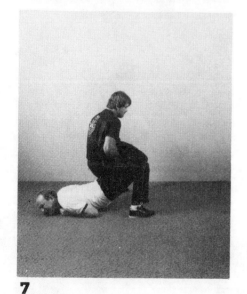

**7**

# Palming to bend-over strangle

Shove your opponent's head back by pushing his chin back with your right palm. Slide your left leg up as you step up with your right leg. At the same time, clasp your arms around his neck. Strangle him as you bend him over your leg.

1

2

3

4

# Palming to reverse head lock

After palming, reach around with your right arm and apply a reverse head lock.

**1**

**2**

**3**

**4**

# Hip throw

Step behind your opponent and throw him over your hip.

**1**

**2**

**3**

# Stomp to push-throw

Raise your leg up and stomp down on your opponent's right foot. Push him to the ground by stepping forward with your right leg. You should keep his right foot pinned to the ground while pushing back and down with your right palm and down with your left hand. Finish him off with a punch to the groin.

**1**

**2**

**3**

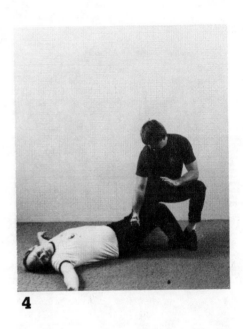

**4**

# Head lock throw

Get your opponent in a head lock and throw him by stepping forward and dropping to one knee.

**1**

**2**

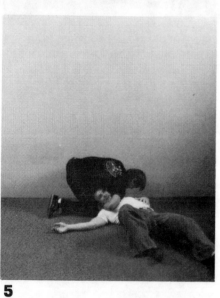

**5**

**3**

**4**

# Reverse double-arm neck throw

Shove your opponent's shoulder back as you push down on his arm. Step up with your rear leg. Pivot around on your right leg and throw him to the ground.

**1**

**2**

**5**

**6**

**3**

**4**

# Underarm hip roll

Step forward and behind your opponent's front leg. Throw him by rolling him over your hip. Control him with a wrist lock or an arm lock.

1

2

5

6

**3**

**4**

The next techniques incorporate a single arm wrap-around.

# Push-shoulder throw

You've wrapped your opponent's left arm and pinned it to your right side. To throw him, push his left shoulder while you pivot to the left. Control him by bending his arm over your leg.

1

2

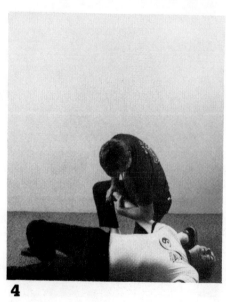

3

4

# Hand choke with leg throw

This time you've wrapped your opponent's right arm and pinned it to your left side. Grab his throat with your right palm as you step behind him with your right leg. Throw him over your leg by shoving his throat.

1

2

3

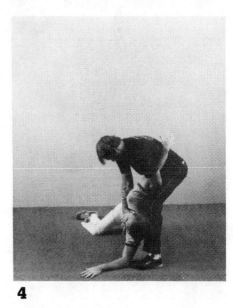

4

# Arm-pin with leg-trip and shoulder-push

Go to a single arm wrap-around with your left arm. Step behind his right leg (with your right leg), and throw him by pushing his right shoulder. Control him with a figure four arm lock.

**1**

**2**

**5**

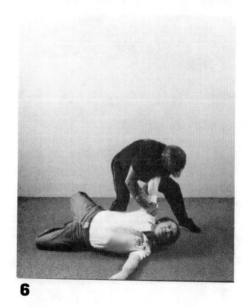

**6**

**3**

**4**

# Underarm hook, and hip throw

Go to a single arm wrap-around. Step behind your opponent's right leg with your right leg and hook your right arm under his left arm. Lift up and throw him over your hip. To control him, lock his arm as you push down on his head.

**1**

**2**

**5**

**6**

**3**

**4**

# Reverse nelson throw

Your opponent's right arm is captured in a wrap-around. Push his head to the right with your left hand as you pull down on his right arm. Step forward with your right leg and throw him. To control him, twist his head.

**1**

**2**

**5**

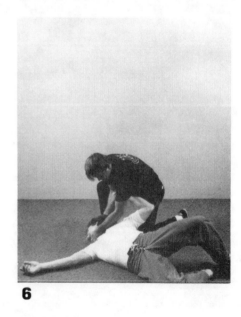

**6**

**3**

**4**

The next sequences use a double arm wrap-around.

# Leg throw

Manipulate your opponent until you can apply a double arm wrap-around. Bring your right leg across your opponent's right leg and throw him over your leg. Control him with an arm lock.

**1**

**2**

**5**

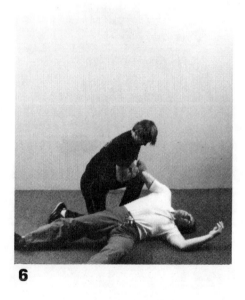

**6**

**3**

**4**

# Head lock hip throw

From a double arm wrap-around, step forward with your right leg and get your opponent in a headlock. Then throw him over your hip. Control him by pressing down on his head and chin.

**1**

**2**

**5**

**3**

**4**

# ABOUT THE AUTHOR

According to Dan Inosanto, Larry Hartsell is one of the premier jeet kune do fighters. Larry started his martial arts training by studying judo in North Carolina from 1957 to 1960. In 1960 Larry moved to California and studied kenpo karate with Ed Parker from 1961 to 1969. Shortly after receiving his black belt in kenpo, he went into the army, serving in Vietnam from 1966, to 1967. After his discharge from the army, Larry was fortunate enough to study jeet kune do from Bruce Lee and Dan Inosanto from 1967 to 1970. When he moved back to North Carolina in 1973, Larry opened up the only authorized jeet kune do school east of California.

Larry has an associate degree in criminology, and ten years of practical experience in law enforcement. He also has had extensive training in boxing and wrestling. Besides teaching in his own school, Larry has taught self-defense tactics and baton to law enforcement officers at Piedmont Central Community College and has worked with the Dallas Cowboys. For the last two summers he has taught at the California Martial Arts Academy at the University of California at Irvine.

Just before writing this book, Larry moved back to California and began teaching his own class at Dan Inosanto's Kali-Jun Fan Academy in Marina Del Rey. Larry also gives private lessons and Jeet Kune Do seminars around the country, as well as running a personal security service.